Revision Tables

The Quick and Easy Way to Exam Success

Companion Notes to the Study Guide for Edexcel IGCSE Anthology Non-Fiction Texts for the English Language Exam

Josephine Pearce

A Study Smart Guide
© Purley Press 2019

Edexcel

International GCSE in English Language
Paper 1 Non-fiction Texts and Transactional Writing
For the Exam

1. **The Danger of a Single Story by Chimamanda Ngozi Adichie**

2. **A Passage to Africa by George Alagiah**

3. **The Explorer's Daughter by Kari Herbert**

4. **Explorers or boys messing about? Either way, taxpayer gets rescue bill by Steven Morris**

5. **Between a Rock and a Hard Place, by Aron Ralston**

6. **Young and dyslexic? You've got it going on by Benjamin Zephaniah**

7. **A Game of Polo with a Headless Goat, by Emma Levine**

8. **Beyond the Sky and the Earth: A Journey into Bhutan, by Jamie Zeppa**

9. **H is for Hawk, by Helen Macdonald**

10. **Chinese Cinderella, by Adeline Yen Mah**

Edexcel

International GCSE in English Language

Paper 1 Non-fiction Texts and Transactional Writing

Exam worth 60% of entire IGCSE in English Language

Content of Exam:

Section A:

There will be a mixture of short and long-answer questions related to a previously unseen non-fiction text which forms a Comprehension.

Next, there will be a question on the methods the writer uses to create an effect on the reader in one of the Prose Anthology articles from Part 1: Paper 1 Section A Non-fiction texts.

Finally, the Prose Anthology Article chosen for the previous question will be compared with the unseen non-fiction text from the Comprehension.

This book is a set of companion notes to be used alongside the "Study Guide for the New Edexcel IGCSE Anthology Non-Fiction Texts for the English Language Exam", also by Josephine Pearce.

Every question on the Prose Anthology section of the Exam requires students to score 12 marks by analysing the methods the writer of one of the extracts uses to create an effect on the reader. In this revision aid, each article is boiled down to named techniques and meanings. Once the article has been understood by using the Study Guide, these notes can be learnt for use in the exam. They are a guarantee of success.

1. The Danger of a Single Story by Chimamanda Ngozi Adichie

MESSAGE: it is hazardous to accept an easy version of the truth without looking around to see the reality.

QUOTE	TECHNIQUE	EFFECT ON THE READER
"I'm a storyteller."	First person narrative voice and short sentence	The statement grabs the reader's attention and establishes Adichie is talking about herself. This is autobiography. It is a firm and commanding opening to show this is a significant moment.
"danger of the single story"	Diction choice of word "danger"	The word "danger" alerts the reader that something very serious is going to be discussed, and this creates suspense for the rest of the passage
"they played in the snow"	Long sentence structure, listing features of characters in her stories	The lengthy list of features which are all western and not like the writer's own experience, creates a layering effect to show how deeply she had been influenced by the books she read to exclude her own life and features.
"Nigeria"	Repetition of proper noun	The name of the country is repeated twice to show the difference between the stories she read and the reality of her home.
"mangoes" and "apples"	Fruit diction	She juxtaposes the names of Western fruit with the tropical fruit she has at home to show the difference between what she read and what she experienced
"mental shift in my perception"	metaphor	The image compares how her mind changes direction with idea of changing gear when driving. It shows that she had to make a conscious change to see the truth.
"stirred my imagination"	metaphor	The image compares her

		imagination to a cup of tea being swirled around by a spoon. This shows how much books excited and influenced her.
"finish your food"	Alliteration of f sound and reported speech	These techniques underline how strongly her mother tells her off for not appreciating Fide's experience.
"I was startled"	Short sentence	The shortness of the sentence highlights the shock that Adichie feels when she discovers that there was more to Fide's life than poverty.
"shocked by her"	Juxtaposition with "startled" of two words meaning surprised	The use of words meaning surprise is effective in showing that while Adichie is surprised by the reality of Fide's life, in turn her American roommate is surprised by the reality of Adichie's life. The diction creates a sense that Adichie is in the same position as her servant, Fide, when she is America
"What struck me was this"	Metaphor of striking or hitting someone	The violent image of being hit by the truth shows how shocking and surprising it was when Adichie realised her roommate felt sorry for her
"patronizing" "pity" and "no possibility"	Alliteration of plosive p sound	This makes a harsh sound to underline how unhappy Adichie is to be stereotyped by her roommate
"a single story of Africa: a single story of catastrophe"	Sentence structure using colon to balance ideas. Word choice of "catastrophe"	Sentence structure uses the colon almost as an equals sign to show that Africa has become equated with disaster in Western stories. The choice of the word "catastrophe" is emotive, making the reader feel it is a country full of terrible things.
"fleecing", "sneaking" and "arrested"	Negative diction	The accumulation of the negative diction is used to show the horrible

		stereotypes which are communicated about Mexicans being untrustworthy and criminal
"I remember"	Verb to remember	This underlines the importance of personal experience to find the truth about a situation.
"stories matter"	Moves from a single story in title to a plural noun "stories"	This shows that there is always more than one story to tell, and that it is important we listen to them all to decide the truth.
"break the dignity" and "repair that broken dignity"	Repetition of the phrase	This is used to show how it is possible for stories to destroy, but also to rebuild.
"a kind of paradise was regained"	Allusion to John Milton's "Paradise Regained" 1671	The allusion refers to Milton's poem which tells how Jesus brings back the possibility of paradise in the afterlife after Adam and Eve lost the Garden of Eden due to original sin. This shows that it is possible through reading to get back to the truth and to see the world in a more positive way.

2. A Passage to Africa by George Alagiah

MESSAGE: The journalist remembers the face of a suffering man who made him rethink his responsibility towards the people he reports on. The extract communicates how important it is to see everyone as an individual so we can remain compassionate.

QUOTE	TECHNIQUE	EFFECT ON THE READER
"I saw"	Past tense, first person narrator	The opening establishes that the piece is personal and is about remembering something important.
"there is one I will never forget"	Refrain – the phrase is repeated throughout the passage	The phrase and its repetition creates suspense for the reader. We want to know what happened, and by repeating the phrase the writer keeps us waiting to hear the answer.
"like a ghost village"	simile	The simile compares a place where people are suffering to a village populated by the dead. This communicates the horror of the place they are going to
"ghoulish", "hunt", "tramped" and "callous"	Word choice of negative adjectives	All these words are negative adjectives to describe how cruel and heartless journalists are in the pursuit of a story. It tells the reader how Alagiah behaved before he saw the face which changed him.
"like the craving for a drug"	simile	The image compares a journalist's search for shocking stories to the desire an addict has for a drug. This communicates that journalists are driven, out of control, and ruthless about getting what they want, just like drug addicts.
"Amina Abdirahman" "Habiba", "Ayaan"	Proper nouns	The use of proper nouns or giving actual names to the victims serves to humanise them for the reader. It makes us more involved and sympathetic.
"no rage, no whimpering…fictionless, motionless"	repetition of negatives	The repetition of "no" and the suffix "less" are used to underline how little fight the dying people have. It shows the reader that they have been so ground down that they can no longer battle to stay alive. This engages the reader's sympathy.

"vision", "smell", "hear and smell"	Sensory descriptions	By using descriptions of how things look, smell and sound, Alagiah underlines the repulsive nature of starvation and death. This is used to shock and engage the reader.
"the gentle V-shape of a boomerang"	metaphor	The image compares the horribly bent old lady's leg with a boomerang. This is a powerful image for a number of reasons. A boomerang is used by aborigines to hunt with, so it suggest that she has been hunted down. A boomerang is also used as a child's toy; this suggests shockingly that the woman's injuries are being made light of or fun of and not taken seriously. Both these interpretations make the image shocking and upsetting.
"a fleeting meeting of eyes"	Assonance and rhyme	The moment Alagiah joins looks with the man is described through a rhyming assonance which not only makes it stand out, but also underlines the beauty and significance of it.
"how could it be?" "What was it about that smile?" "so strong and confident?"	questions	The writer uses a series of questions to show his confusion about why the suffering man smiles as him. This shows that he is really influenced by the moment and is about to learn something from it.
"The journalist observes, the subject is observed. The journalist is active, the subject is passive"	Listing of binary oppositions	The writer lists a series of opposites or antithetical words to show that the relationship between the West and Third World is one which constantly places on as superior and one as inferior. He does this to show the reader that we should question this relationship and try to see these countries differently.
"But this smile had turned the tables."	Opening sentence with conjunction. metaphor	By opening the sentence with a conjunction, which is not grammatically correct, the writer highlights that his normally formal thinking processes have been thrown into chaos by this moment. The metaphor of turning the

		tables comes from backgammon when a player finds themselves swapped into the position of their opponent. The image suggests that the writer has changed places with the people he writes about. This shows how influential the moment is to him.
"So, my nameless friend, if you are still alive, I owe you one."	Colloquial expression Oxymoron Idiomatic phrase	"So" is a colloquial expression suggesting a summary. This shows the writer has come to a conclusion and is expressing it in an informal way to engage the reader. "Nameless friend" is an oxymoron or two contradictory terms lashed together. This shows the conflictual relationship the writer is in with the man who influenced him as he does not really know him. "I owe you one" is an idiomatic phrase usually used to express that a person will buy a drink for a friend as repayment for a favour. This image shows that the writer has become indebted to his subject. This is a different relationship from the one he began the extract with. Alagiah has had an epiphany, realising that the people he reports on are more important than he is.

3. The Explorer's Daughter by Kari Herbert

MESSAGE: The extract considers the dilemma of hunting endangered species. The ultimate message of the passage is that when killing rare animals is essential to being able to carry on living in difficult environments, it should be allowed.

QUOTE	TECHNIQUE	EFFECT ON THE READER
"Two hours after the last of the hunters had returned and eaten"	Use of time as a marker	Throughout the passage time is repeatedly mentioned to create a feeling of immediacy, as though the events are happening now and are therefore even more important.
"Catching the light in a spectral play of colour"	Adjective choice - spectral	Spectral means like a spectre or ghost. Thus the description suggests that the narwhals are somehow supernatural and extraordinary, creating an extreme sense of drama
"slowly, methodically"	Choice of adverbs	The two adverbs are used to describe the slow and deliberate progress of the narwhals, creating tension and suspense as to what will happen next.
"glittering kingdom" "glinting off man and whale" "butter-gold"	Visual description	The environment is repeatedly described in golden terms. The creates an impression of not only the beauty of the animals and hunters, but also the wealth and importance of their endeavours.
"the narwhal is an essential contributor to the survival of the hunters"	Tense changes from past to present	The change of tense from past to the present indicates the passage is now providing factual information. This also underlines the idea that this information is not personal, like the description of the hunt.
"mattak" "scurvy"	Expert diction	The passage uses specific diction from the culture of the country and from medicine. This gives the passage a rational and factual atmosphere which helps the writer to persuade the reader that hunting is a necessity.
"pointing" "focusing" "occasionally spinning"	Present participles	A series of present participles are used to create a sense of the ongoing frenzied activity of the women who are watching the men hunt. It underlines how tense the situation is.
"It was like watching a vast, waterborne game with the	Two similes	The first simile compares the hunt to something the reader

hunters spread out like a net around the sound."		can relate to – a game on the water. However, the image is deliberately jarring as this is not a game, and either man or whale will be killed. The second simile compares the formation of the hunters to net thrown across the water. It suggests how connected the men are, and also how organised they are.
"He gently picked up his harpoon and aimed – in that split second my heart leapt for both hunter and narwhal."	Adverb – "gently" Punctuation – dash Sibilance – "split second" Personification – "heart leapt"	The passage focuses on the battle between one hunter and one whale to make the debate about hunting more personal. The adverb "gently" suggests the movement of the hunter is graceful. This makes us sympathetic to him, even though he is hunting. The dash slows down the sentence to force the reader to think about this moment and the choice between killing and saving the whale. The sibilance creates a hushed moment for the reader to dwell on the frozen moment of the hunt. The personification of the writer's heart jumping in her chest because of the tension of the moment creates suspense for the reader. We wonder how this battle will end.
"I urged the man on in my head" "at the same time my heart also urged the narwhal to dive, to leave, to survive"	Juxtaposition of head and heart Listing of infinitive verbs	The writer juxtaposes the images of head and heart to show that she rationally encourages the hunter, but emotionally wishes the whale could survive. The juxtaposition encapsulates the dilemma or choice between hunting to live, and killing endangered animals. The list of three infinitive verbs which are all about escape suggests how much the writer wants the whale to survive. By being in the infinitive the verbs have no tense. This means the dilemma is left frozen outside time for the reader to imagination and decide how it should end.
"I understand the harshness of	Present tense	The passage moves back to the

life in the Arctic and the needs of the hunters and their families to hunt"	First person narrative voice Factual information	present tense to show the writer is going to provide more factual information. The first person narrative voice shows that she is expressing her own opinion here.
"How can you possibly eat seal?"	Rhetorical question	The writer uses the rhetorical question which she does not answer to show how tricky the debate is about hunting
"the images that bombarded us"	metaphor	The writer compares the way the pictures of hunting seals were communicated to bombardment which is a military term, meaning heavily bombed. This suggests that the public is being manipulated wrongly by the media's emotive images.
"do not kill seals using this method, nor do they kill for sport."	Use of two negatives Repetition of verb to kill	The use of the negatives shows the writer is underlining that the Greenlanders do not kill in an unnecessary or cruel way. This is trying to persuade the reader. However, the writer uses the word "kill" twice to show she is not shying away from what is happening, even though she is defending it. This is designed to influence the reader's opinion on hunting.
"Hunting is still an absolute necessity in Thule"	Clear conclusion and answer	The passage ends with a short sentence expressing the writer's opinion on the importance of hunting for survival. It is not ambiguous. She gives a clear answer to the dilemma.

4. Explorers or Boys Messing about? Either way, taxpayer gets rescue bill by Steven Morris

MESSAGE: The newspaper article communicates through amusing and subtle implications that the two wealthy playboy explorers are reckless, selfish and dangerous, and that we should mock them.

QUOTE	TECHNIQUE	EFFECT ON THE READER
"Explorers or boys messing about?"	Rhetorical question Diction choice – noun and verb	The writer's title employs a rhetorical question. This technique is used to persuade the reader. The question makes the reader think about the point, but the wording of it suggests which side the writer belongs to. The noun "boys" is highly derogatory, making the grown up explorers sound like children, while the verb "messing" suggests an activity which is not serious. These words communicate what Morris thinks while pretending to offer the reader a choice.
"farce" "tragedy" "drama"	Theatre diction	The writer describes the expedition with a number of terms related to the theatre. This suggests that what they are doing is not real, but a play. Moreover, the terms are quite negative. A "farce" is an exaggerated comedy, while a "tragedy" is a highly serious tale ending in downfall, and a "drama" is something not real, but entertaining to watch. Together the terms persuade the reader that the men have been doing something playful and silly.
"their helicopter plunged" "The men were plucked"	Repetition of plosive sounding verbs	The repetition of plosive sounding verbs such as "plunged" and "plucked" creates the impression of a violent impact. This communicates what the crash must have been like.
"The men were plucked from the icy water"	Verb choice	By describing the manner in which the explorers were saved with the verb "plucked", the writer makes them sound tiny and insignificant. Something which can be plucked is usually small and feeble. This ridicules the men.
"in some quarters"	Vague phrasing	The writer suggests without being explicit that some

		sources are criticising the men. This communicates that their actions are disapproved of.
"Experts question the wisdom"	Use of word expert	The writer uses the word "expert" in order to suggest that the men are not professional or expert.
"also known as Q"	Allusion to character Q in Bond films Use of comedy	The writer notes Mr Smith's nickname, "Q" in order to make fun of it. It alludes to the Bond films where Q is the Quartermaster who supplies the clever gadgets. In this case, their clever gadgets have failed.
"HMS Endurance"	Allusion to HMS Endurance 1914 ship which Sir Ernest Shackelton used to go to south pole and where he lost the ship, but saved all the men through great leadership	The allusion to Shackleton's ship diminishes and belittles the explorers as they are not as brave as the great captain.
"nothing short of a miracle"	Biblical image	Mr Brooks' wife compares her husband's survival with a miracle, showing that only something supernatural could have saved them. This suggests that the expedition was very dangerous.
"experienced adventurers"	Adjective irony	The choice of the adjective "experienced" is ironic here, because the writer is pointing out that they should have known better than do something this dangerous.
"survived a charge by a silver back gorilla"	hyperbole	The writer lists a number of adventures the men have had which are exaggerated to make fun of them.
"They'll probably have their bottoms kicked and be sent home the long way"	metaphor	The image compares the men to school boys who have been punished. This diminishes them and makes them seem comic.

5. Between a Rock and a Hard Place by Aron Ralston

MESSAGE: The passage communicates the importance of making difficult decisions. It suggests that human beings can make remarkable sacrifices to survive.

QUOTE	TECHNIQUE	EFFECT ON THE READER
"I come to another drop-off"	First person singular narrative voice Present tense Technical climbing diction	The use of the first person underlines the intimate, autobiographical nature of the passage. The present tense means that the passage is happening as we read it. This makes it immediate, dramatic and tense. The technical diction of climbing shows the reader that the writer is an expert at this, making what happens next even more awful.
"refrigerator chockstone"	metaphor	The stone is compared to a refrigerator to communicate the size and weight of it. This helps the reader to understand an experience they might not have had.
"claustrophobic" "slot" "narrows to a consistent three feet across"	Repetition of diction referring to confined spaces	Claustrophobia is the fear of closed spaces. This adjective tells the reader how small the tunnel is. This detail is then layered with more references to the narrowing of the tunnel. This creates a worrying sense of being trapped.
"Sometimes in narrow passages like this one"	Digression Technical expertise	The second paragraph digresses or moves away from the subject of the first, to tell us about climbing generally, and to explain technical details of the sport. This communicates the writer's expertise, making his later accident seem unavoidable.
"you can imagine using it to climb up the inside of a chimney"	Direct address, using second person	The use of "you" means the writer is directly speaking to the reader. This involves us in his experience and makes us more empathetic to him.
"a chockstone the size of a large bus tire."	metaphor	The metaphor compares the rock to a bus tyre. This gives the reader an idea of the size and weight of the stone which makes it relatable.
"If I can step onto it, then I'll have a nine-foot height to descend"	Future tense	The passage moves into the future tense. This gives the reader the impression that the writer is working out how to do the next part of the climb. This creates great tension as the reader is drawn into his decisions, and feels we are experiencing the accident with him.
"I'll dangle off the chockstone"	Choice of verb	The verb "dangle" is precarious. It suggests that the writer is going to move in a way which is

		dangerous. This creates suspense for the reader.
"Stemming across the canyon at the lip of the drop-off"	Present tense	The use of the present participle, "stemming" returns the passage to the present tense. We experience the action as if it is happening now, making it dramatic and very tense.
"Instantly, I know this is trouble, and instinctively, I let go"	Alliteration Repetition of adverbs	The repeated "I" sound of "instantly" and "instinctively" reinforce each other, drawing attention to the writer's reaction. The adverbs describe how the writer reacts quickly and almost without thought. This puts the reader inside the writer's head, showing the details of how the accident happened, making it very dramatic and tense.
"consumes the sky"	Personification and metaphor	The falling stone is personified as something which eats up the sky above the writer. The image is aggressive and frightening. The stone has come to life and seems to be attacking him. This makes the accident seem even more horrifying.
"the next three seconds" "Time dilates, as if I'm dreaming, and my reactions decelerate"	References to time Simile Use of extended syllables	The repeated references to the slowness of time are used to show how the accident feels. The simile "as if I'm dreaming" compares the experience to something unreal and dreamlike. This is a feeling the reader can understand. The three clauses in the sentence each get longer – 3 syllables; 5 syllables, then 9 syllables. The lengthening of the sentence mirrors the way time feels for the writer now he is trapped.
"smashes" "collision" "yank" "rock ricochets" "crushes"	Series of verbs	The verbs in this section are all violent. This underlines how aggressive and awful the accident is. A "collision" usually describes something crashing, while "ricochets" is usually applied to bullets bouncing off bodies. The verbs together create a network of violent description, communicating the horror of the situation.
"ensnares my right arm"	Personification and metaphor	The image compares the rock holding the writer's arm to an animal being caught in a trap or snare. This makes the rock active and aggressive, creating a drama between the writer and stone which is his enemy.
"flaring agony"	metaphor	The metaphor compares the sudden pain of the accident to something which immediately

		flares up or explodes. The image is violent and horrifying, communicating how the writer felt.
"I grimace and growl"	Alliteration and onomatopoeia	The alliteration of "gr" sound creates the sound of a growl in the reader's head. This communicates the intense pain the writer is feeling, creating drama, tension and empathy.
"Anxiety has my brain tweaking"	Slang metaphor	The word "tweaking" is American slang. It is comparing the writer's thoughts to those of a crack addict going desperate to get a hit of the drug. Therefore the pain the writer is feeling is disorientating and painful, like a drug addict denied drugs.
"right now"	Use of italics	The italics emphasize the importance and emotion of the words. Here this is communicating that this moment is the writer's best chance to escape.
"Nothing"	One word sentence Negative word	The passage ends with a one word sentence. The shortness of the expression communicates the desperation and loss of hope the writer feels. The word "Nothing" tells the reader that the writer cannot move the rock. He is trapped. This leaves the reader with a terrible sense of hopelessness and despair.

6. Young and dyslexic? You've got it going on by Benjamin Zephaniah

MESSAGE: The passage suggests that people who are dyslexic are prejudiced against in the same way as black people are. It concludes that both black people and dyslexics are actually very talented and should recognise how exceptional they are.

QUOTE	TECHNIQUE	EFFECT ON THE READER
"you've got it going on"	American colloquialism	The use of American slang immediately makes the article seem colloquial, friendly and accessible. The phrase means if you are young and dyslexic then you have extraordinary talents.
"As a child I suffered"	First person singular narrative voice	The use of first person singular makes the passage very personal and autobiographical. This engages the reader.
"We are the architects, we are the designers"	First person plural narrative voice Sentence structure of repetition	By moving to the first person plural, "We", the writer embraces the readers who are also dyslexic, making the passage friendly and inclusive. The repetitive sentence structure which creates a list of things dyslexics are good at underlines the talents of dyslexics.
"there was no compassion, no understanding and no humanity"	Repetition of no	The repetition of the negative "no" three times emphasizes how little care was given to dyslexics when the writer was at school.
"Shut up, stupid boy."	Direct speech sibilance	The teacher's response to the writer's excellent idea about sleep is given in direct speech to make it more brutal, aggressive and immediate. The repeated sibilant "s" sounds add to the effect of hissing out an aggressive put down. This makes the reader sympathetic to the experiences of the writer.
"local savages"	Choice of adjective	By using the adjective "savages" to describe Africans, the teacher shows how racist language is. A savage is someone uncivilised and wild. This is a racist stereotype which the writer gets in trouble for pointing out. This begins a process in the article of juxtaposing the unfair treatment of black people with

		the unfair treatment of dyslexics. This is done to reinforce how terrible prejudice against dyslexics is.
"for being a rude boy"	British colloquialism	The use of the British slang term "rude boy," which means gangster, makes the article seem up-to-date and relatable for the reader. This engages the reader.
"But I think staying out of prison"	Opening sentence with a conjunction	By opening the sentence ungrammatically, with a conjunction, the writer is indicating that something important and out of the ordinary happened. He is showing that he made an decision to be different.
"But I think staying out of prison is about conquering your fears and finding your path in life."	metaphors	The writer uses two metaphors. He compares staying out of prison to a battle in which he has had to "conquer" his fears. This underlines how hard he has had to fight to be who he is. The second metaphor compare staying out of prison with a journey on which you have to take the correct "path". This again shows how the writer has had to make conscious decisions about the course his life will take. This is highly admirable and is setting an example for the reader to follow.
"opportunities opened for me"	metaphor	The writer compares how he was lucky enough to find options with a door opening. The image shows that in life there are always open doors, and people must make the right decision to go through them. This underlines the hope there is for dyslexics.
Do I need an operation?	Noun choice	The writer expresses how little was known about dyslexia through his reaction to being told his condition. By calling it an "operation" the writer shows that people mistakenly think it is an illness and something negative, whereas actually it can suggest a special talent.
"if you don't have passion,	Triplet of abstract nouns	The writer uses a triplet of

		abstract nouns to indicate the qualities that being dyslexic gives an individual. Each on is a great talent, which proves how extraordinary and valuable dyslexics are.
"if someone oppresses me because of my race I don't sit down and think, 'How can I become white?' It's not my problem, its theirs.	Conditional sentence Rhetorical question	The writer uses a conditional sentence, one beginning with "if" to show that just because one fact is true it does not mean that there is an obvious consequence. Here he says if someone is racist to him, it does not make him think he should try to become white. He uses a rhetorical question to persuade the reader how silly it would be to try to change his skin colour. The writer is juxtaposing racism with prejudice towards dyslexics. Both forms of discrimination are unfair. Moreover, the writer is suggesting that just because some people in society are prejudiced towards dyslexics should not mean that dyslexics should want to stop being themselves. He is again saying that dyslexics have their own talents to be proud of and should change for no one.
"so don't be heavy on yourself"	Colloquial term	The term "heavy" is a friendly, colloquial term meaning a feeling of weighty seriousness that makes a person feel stressed and unhappy. The writer is using the term to show the reader, in an accessible way, that there is nothing wrong with being dyslexic and not to worry about it.
"your 'creative muscle' gets bigger"	metaphor	The writer uses a metaphor to compare the process of getting better at being creative with lifting weights to make your muscles bigger. The metaphor brings together the brain and the body in a clever way which makes the idea visual and relatable.
"We are the architects. We are the designers"	refrain	The writer uses a refrain or repeated phrase from the opening of the article to conclude it. This frames and

		reiterates his point to reinforce what talented people dyslexics are.
"Bloody non-dyslexics…who do they think they are?"	Swear word Rhetorical question humour	The writer ends the passage with a rhetorical question which makes non-dyslexics think about what talents they have by comparison to the extraordinary dyslexics. The use of a swear word makes the sentence forceful, but also humorous. The writer ends the article with a direct challenge to non-dyslexics, making them wonder about their own behaviour and abilities. This reinforces the idea of the writer embracing dyslexics and making those who have alienated them feel what it is like to be singled out.

7. A Game of Polo with a Headless Goat by Emma Levine

MESSAGE: The description of the unusual sport of donkey racing is employed to communicate to the reader the fun of activities which we do not know.

QUOTE	TECHNIQUE	EFFECT ON THE READER
"We drove off to find the best viewing spot"	First person plural narrative voice	By writing in the first person Levine shows that the passage is about a personal experience. However, she also uses the plural form, "we". This enables her to communicate that she is part of a group. More importantly, it involves the reader in the story, making us feel a part of her experience, and thereby communicating the fun it is.
"I asked the lads of we could join in the 'Wacky Races'"	Colloquial language Allusion	The writer calls her team "the lads" which is a colloquial or slang expression. This chatty tone makes the passage seem entertaining and friendly. Also by calling her colleagues, "lads" she makes them seem enjoyable company and approachable for the reader. She also alludes to the children's cartoon "Wacky Races" which is a hilarious depiction of a race between a number of comic animated characters. This compares the donkey race to something the reader can understand, and something they know indicates it is a funny and entertaining activity. This sets the tone of the passage.
"We waited for eternity on the brow of the hill" "Nearly one hour later"	References to time	The writer employs multiple references to waiting and time to communicate a sense of suspense to the reader. This makes us also look forward to the race arriving.
"me perched in the boot"	Verb choice	The choice of "perch" describes the writer's position in the car boot as being like a bird sitting on a branch. This underlines how physically precarious and potentially dangerous this could be.
"fifty vehicles roaring up in their wake"	Personification and metaphor	The vehicles are personified in a metaphor comparing them to an animal that roars, such as a lion. This creates tension and excitement as the crowd is fiercely in pursuit of the donkeys.
"The two donkeys were almost dwarfed by their entourage"	Verb choice Word choice	By choosing the verb to dwarf, the writer underlines in a comic way how small the donkeys are in comparison to the crowds following them. She describes the crowds as "entourage". This is a

		specific word, meaning the group of people who surround an important person. The word comes from Hollywood and is used to make the race understandable to the reader.
"using their whips energetically, although not cruelly."	Use of adverb	By using the adverb "energetically" to describe how the riders whip the donkeys, Levine is trying to persuade the reader that the race is not cruel to animals and is just a fun activity.
"Kibla donkey is said to achieve speeds of up to 40kph"	Factual information	The writer includes informative facts about the donkeys to show that she is also educating the reader, as well as entertaining them.
"horns tooting, bells ringing, and the special rattles"	Sense of hearing Listing of noises Onomatopoeia	The writer lists a series of noises made during the race. The use of the sense of hearing makes the race seem very vivid and real to the reader. The sounds are also onomatopoeic; "tooting" sounds like the noise the horns make. The writer successfully communicates a vibrant scene to the reader.
"This was Formula One without rules"	Allusion Metaphor	The writer makes an allusion to a sport that her readers will understand and know. By comparing the donkey race to Formula One car racing, the writer creates a comic juxtaposition between a very fast and wealthy sport, and the much slower donkeys. Again, this underlines how fun the sport is.
"it was survival of the fittest"	allusion	The phrase alludes to Charles Darwin's Origin of Species which suggests that animals evolve over time with the least fit dying out and only those with the healthiest attributes breeding and continuing. The comparison between the drivers who can keep up with the donkeys and Darwin's theory is again comic. It makes the race sound more dangerous than it is for humorous effect.
"Ahead of the donkeys, oncoming traffic – for it was a main road – had to dive into the ditch"	Punctuation – dashes Alliteration metaphor	The writer breaks up her sentence with dashes instead of commas to show the fast pace of the race, and how much needs to be described. The alliteration of the d sound underlines the verb "to dive" indicating how the cars have to hurtle down into the ditch to avoid the race. Again this communicates pace and fun.
"The race was over"	Short sentence	The shortness of the sentence suggests or mirrors the fact that

		the race has been cut short by an accident. It creates a sense of disappointment in the reader and surprise.
"there were over a hundred punters"	Colloquial diction	The word "punters" is a colloquial word to describe people who gamble on an event. Again, this makes the passage understandable to the reader, and also quite chatty and light hearted.
"Voices were raised, fists were out and tempers rising"	Listing	The race breaks down into an argument about who won. The writer uses a list technique to describe the increasing aggression. She employs a series of the verb "to raise" twice: "raised" "rising" to show how the argument is getting more out of hand. The potential violence of the situation is quickly glossed over to keep the tone light and entertaining.
"But I don't even have my licence yet because I'm underage!"	Direct speech	The driver's confession that he is driving illegally and is too young is treated as comic here. The writer is keen to maintain a light-hearted tone.
"A massive pile-up in the middle of the high-stakes donkey race could have caused problems."	Litotes or understatement	The writer ends the passage with another comic moment. She imagines the trouble that could have been caused had her illegal driver crashed, using a phrase which understates the real dangers of the situation. This ends the extract on a moment of humour.

8. Beyond the Sky and the Earth: A Journey into Bhutan by Jamie Zeppa

MESSAGE: The passage communicates that the country of Bhutan is a beautiful and civilised place which has been negatively affected by visitors from the west. It suggests that the country should be preserved without interference from the outside world.

QUOTE	TECHNIQUE	EFFECT ON THE READER
"climbing" "rolling"	Present participles	Present participles are neither past nor future. They suggest that the landscape is ancient and persistent. They create a sense of the strangeness and wonder of where she is going.
"to picture a giant child"	metaphor	The writer expresses how unusual the landscape is by saying it could only be made by a large infant playing with it.
"It is my first night"	First person singular Present tense	The account is in the first person to show that this is a personal and autobiographical account. Because it is in the present tense, the words give us the impression that we are experiencing the journey with the writer now.
"I am exhausted, but I cannot sleep"	Short sentence	The shortness of the sentence expresses the length of the writer's journey and her tiredness
"baked-brown" "wind-sharpened"	Compound adjectives – formed by joining two adjectives together	The writer uses these to show that she cannot easily come up with words unless she invents them to express the appearance of the country
"convulsion of crest and gorges"	metaphor	Writer compares the landscape to a convulsion or fit. This suggests it is violently thrown together.
"instant coffee" "powdered milk"	Negative adjectives	The writer uses a number of negative adjectives to describe her breakfast to show that she is shocked and disappointed by the food she is given.
"cultural infiltration"	metaphor	The writer lists a number of western objects such as Rambo posters and jeans and calls them "cultural infiltration". This metaphor suggests the west is deliberately penetrating the country with its culture in order to corrupt it.
"Bhutanese-ness"	Neologism or invented word	The writer invents her own word to describe something she thinks is typical of the country.

		Again it shows that the she thinks the country is very unique and difficult to describe.
"Best built race of men I ever saw"	Quotes a traveller from 1774, George Bogle	By referring to the words of other travellers, the writer wants to provide evidence to support her opinion on the attractiveness of the people.
"Land of the Thunder Dragon"	Past tense information	Writer moves to past tense to describe the history of the country. This provides information, showing how important she thinks the country is.
"a nasty turn"	Bathos or understatement to create humour	The writer describes the relationship between the British and Bhutan using a phrase which understates and makes fun of the difficult situation.
"Great Game"	metaphor	Writer uses a metaphor for the way the great powers of Britain and Russia fought to dominate Asia in 19thC. The metaphor of their activity being like a game shows that they did not take seriously the fates of the people of these countries. The writer is ironically highlighting the serious trouble caused by external nations fighting over these countries.

9. H is for Hawk by Helen Macdonald

MESSAGE: The passage communicates the struggle to overcome bereavement by forging a new relationship with a hawk.

QUOTE	TECHNIQUE	EFFECT ON THE READER
"'Don't want you going home with the wrong bird'"	Direct speech In media res Proleptic	The passage opens in media res or in the middle of the action to create excitement. The first words are direct speech which instils a sense of action and immediacy. The cautionary words about avoiding going home with the wrong bird are proleptic or looking to the future. This sets up a suspicion in the reader's mind. By the end of the article, the reader realises that the 'wrong' bird is actually the 'right bird for the writer.
"A sudden *thump* of feathered shoulders and the box shook as if someone had punched it"	Italics Onomatopoeia simile	The italicised "thump" makes the word seem more violent and forceful which communicates the nature of the bird in the box. The word thump is onomatopoeic, sounding like the action of hitting. The simile compares the sound to someone punching the box. These techniques create a sense of foreboding and dread at what is inside the box.
"concentration. Infinite caution. Daylight irrigating the box."	Short incomplete sentences	A series of short incomplete sentences are used to communicate the pace, excitement, and anticipation at the moment the bird is going to be revealed.
"Daylight irrigating the box"	metaphor	The verb to irrigate means to flood with water. Here it is used to describe the sunlight pouring into the bird's box. The image is effective because it is strange. The mixing of a water image with a description of light shows the senses of the writer are so alert at this moment that they are confused and intertwined. This creates excitement and engagement in the reader.
"the man pulls an enormous, enormous hawk out of the box"	Change to present tense repetition	The passage changes from the past tense to the present tense. This makes it seem to the reader as though the events are happening now. The repetition of enormous communicates the shock the writer feels at the size and appearance of the hawk she has bought.
"her feathers raised like the scattered quills of a fretful porpentine"	simile	The bird's jagged feathers are compared in the simile to the spikes of a porcupine. This image

		makes the bird appear aggressive and violent. It is frightening.
"she is a conjuring trick"	metaphor	The bird is compared in the metaphor to a magical illusion. This suggests the animal is supernatural and frightening.
"A reptile, a fallen angel. A griffon"	Listing of proper nouns	The process of listing different things to identify what the bird is suggests that the animal is impossible to comprehend. This shows the writer is horrified by the bird. The things the bird is compared with are also startling. A reptile or lizard sounds unpleasant; a fallen angel is a devil and therefore evil, while a griffon is a mythical creature with the body of a lion and the head of an eagle. Each of these names suggests the bird is horrifying, powerful, malevolent.
"But now it is this; and she can see everything…"	Long sentence Starting with conjunction	The long sentence which runs over five lines describes the things the bird sees now it out of the box. By giving us the bird's point of view the reader is able to see how remarkable the bird is and how much she enjoys freedom. By starting the sentence with a conjunction which is not grammatically correct, the writer is showing how horrifying the startling the situation is for the bird.
"All at once I loved this man, and fiercely."	adverb	The writer imagines how the man has raised the hawk from an egg and it moves her. Her own father has just died, and she is getting the hawk to find friendship and comfort in her grief. The adverb "fiercely" shows that she loves the man's care for the bird in a wild and intense way, like an animal. This shows she like her paternal care, and that she is more like a bird than a human.
"*Oh*"	One word sentence and paragraph Exclamatory word Italics	When the writer discovers the bird is not the one intended for her, the one word paragraph, "Oh" in italics expresses how sad she feels. The writer had engaged with the bird and empathised with its awkward and fearful behaviour in the outside world, because it reminded her of herself dealing with her grief.
"And dear God, it did"	Starting sentence with conjunction profanity	The writer starts the sentence ungrammatically, with a conjunction to show that she is horrified by the bird that is meant to be hers. The profane

		blasphemy of "dear God" shows she needs divine help to deal with this creature. This creates engagement and empathy with the reader.
"she came out like a Victorian melodrama: a sort of madwoman in the attack."	Simile Metaphor Allusion Pun	The bird is first compared to a Victorian melodrama or play with extreme emotion. This means the bird is expressing intense and frightening feelings. The metaphor of the madwoman in the attack alludes to Charlotte Bronte's "Jane Eyre" where the protagonist's groom is hiding his mad first wife in the attic. Here the phrase is punned on to create "madwoman in the attack". This suggests that the bird is not only insane, it is also very aggressive and wants to attack and hurt others. These images create the impression that the bird is full of negative emotions and aggression.
"great awful gouts of sound like a thing in pain"	Metaphor simile	The sound of the bird is compared to gouts. A gout is usually a clot of blood. Here the physical description is used to imagine a sound. This makes the noise of the bird appear to be thick and bloody. It is a horrifying image. The writer adds to it by saying the sound resembles something in terrible pain. Again the writer is communicating the horrifying nature of the second bird.
"crazy barrage of incoherent appeals"	adjective	A barrage is a military word meaning under constant attack. This shows how vehemently the writer appeals to the man to give her the first bird and not the one intended for her. This shows the writer's desperation and creates empathy with the reader.
"With wind-wrecked hair and exhausted eyes"	alliteration	The alliteration of w and then e here underlines how stressed and upset the writer is about trying to get the bird she connects with. The description of her is engaging and sympathetic. It is also makes her like the birds, as another wild animal who is desperate.
"as if she were in a seaside production of Medea"	Allusion simile	The writer compares herself to Medea. This alludes to the Greek play by Euripides in which Medea is so upset by her lover, Jason, deserting her for another woman, she kills their children to spite him. The writer is suggesting that she has also been driven insane with emotion for love. This could be the love of the new bird or the

		love of her dead father. The image is a frighteningly honest one which engages the reader. We feel sorry for how upset and out of control the writer has become.
"The was a moment of total silence".	Cliff hanger	The passage ends without hearing whether the man will give her the bird she wants. This is a cliff hanger or moment of suspense for the reader to create tension and anticipation.

10. Chinese Cinderella by Adeline Yen Mah

MESSAGE: The passage suggests that even after great hardship and oppression, dreams can come true.

QUOTE	TECHNIQUE	EFFECT ON THE READER
"The radio warned of a possible typhoon the next day"	Pathetic fallacy – when the weather reflects the emotions of the characters	The typhoon or tropical storm suggests that there is an impending moment of chaos and turmoil. This establishes anxiety for the reader at the beginning of the passage, making us concerned that something terrible is about to happen.
"I threw the dice" "Monopoly"	metaphor	The game of Monopoly and the throwing of the dice are metaphors in the passage to remind the reader of the importance of chance and luck. The imagery suggests that the writer is at a moment when her luck could change for the better or worse. When she is playing the game, she is losing, which implies that the rest of the passage might be negative too.
"the thought of leaving school throbbed at the back of my mind like a persistent toothache"	simile	The simile compares the idea of leaving school (which most students relish) to a constant, aching pain, such as toothache. This suggests that the writer is experiencing chronic low-level emotional pain and anxiety because what waits for her outside school is so awful. This creates tension and surprise in the reader as we want to know what she dreads and why.
"shrugging his shoulders"	sibilance	The sibilance underlines the rudeness of the chauffeur who is dismissive towards the writer. This is surprising. We expect a member of her family's staff to be courteous to her. Again this suggests that she does not have a good relationship with her family.
"foolishly" "Timidly"	adverbs	The writer uses a series of negative adverbs to describe herself, suggesting that she has low self esteem. She thinks her behaviour is silly and fearful. This engages the reader as we feel sorry for her.
"This is your new home. Your parents moved here a few months ago."	dialogue	The chauffeur reveals that the writer's parents have moved house without telling her. This fact makes the reader increasingly concerned for her as it is clear her family neglect her.
"I had been summoned by Father to enter the Holy of Holies"	allusion	The Holy of Holies is a reference to the Old Testament and the

		Jewish Torah or veiled inner sanctuary of the Tabernacle where God dwelt along with the Ark of the Covenant containing the Ten Commandments. This allusion suggests that the writer's father is like the Old Testament God to her: full of rules and very frightening.
"Is this a giant ruse on his part to trick me?"	Rhetorical questions	The questions show that the writer is confused by what is happening and has never expected to be called to her father. The fact she thinks this could be a "ruse" or action intended to deceive her also underlines that she does not trust that her father wants the best for her.
"Sit down! Sit down!"	Exclamation Imperative sentences Repetition	The repeated commands tell the reader that the writer's father is a bullying and commanding parent who treats her aggressively. This makes us feel sorry for her.
"Is it possible? Am I dreaming? Me, the winner?	Short paragraph Triplet of three questions	The short paragraph expresses how shocked the writer is to have won something. This show how low her self esteem is, making the reader feel sorry for her. The fact it is a triplet of three questions underlines the writer's confusion as having achieved something. She cannot believe that she could do well. Again, this engages our sympathies.
"I had given him face"	Idiomatic phrase metaphor	The phrase is an idiomatic Chinese saying, meaning that a person has been given status in the eyes of another. This image shows that the writer's father is only pleased with her because her success has brought praise to him. This shows how self centred he is.
"I only had to stretch out my hand to reach the stars."	metaphor	The image compares the writer's delight at being praised by her father to touching something impossible and beautiful. This shows the reader how difficult it is to please the writer's father.
"Going to England is like entering heaven."	simile	The image compares the writer's escape to England with entering paradise. This is positive. This shows the reader how much the writer wants to escape her family.
"Writer! He scoffed"	verb choice	The verb to scoff means to laugh at someone. Therefore the diction shows the reader that the writer's father is mocking her idea of becoming a writer. This shows what an unpleasant man he is, and engages the reader to feel sorry for the writer.
"a foolproof profession for you"	Adjective choice	The expression "foolproof" means

		that even idiots will not muck it up. The father is saying that the writer is an idiot who should be able to get right helping women to have babies.
"Bliss was it in that dawn to be alive."	allusion	The quote comes from William Wordsworth's poem "French Revolution" which describes the joy of freedom felt by the French when they rid themselves of an oppressive ruling class. This shows the reader that the writer feels as though she has been tyrannized by her family and is now going to be able to liberate herself.

Printed in Great Britain
by Amazon